PAPER: +METAL

A Radical Juxtaposition of Materials

SANDY BLEIFER

PAPER: +Metal
A Radical Juxtaposition of Materials

ISBN: 978-1-7330719-7-0
Library of Congress Control Number: 2019908220

PAPER: +Metal
A Radical Juxtaposition of Materials

The Metal/Drawings juxtapose the inherent qualities of metal and paper: hardness v. softness, strength v. vulnerability. The drawings are on newsprint, which darkens and becomes even more brittle over time. Burning the paper to produce ash makes the paper even more fragile. Nevertheless, the drawings cling to their metal supports while the metal continues to rust at a slow pace. Rusted metal is a recurrent foil to the qualities of paper in Bleifer's ongoing work.

Book Design and Editing by Debbie Zeitman

Published by Sandy Bleifer / Bleifer InPrint

www.sandybleifer.com

+METAL

Metal juxtaposed with paper to symbolize
the impact of outside forces on the human condition.

Beginning in the 1980s my work became more sculptural and much of it emulated metal surfaces. In a desire to explore working directly with metal, I chose to learn welding and found myself drawn to the scraps available to the students. Using them as a support and as a foil to my work in paper led to the Metal / Drawing series.

The metal that I selected was neither new nor perfect but battered and weather beaten. Because I was working through a very traumatic experience in my life, I used my own blood on some of the drawings. In a very short period of time, the blood completely disappeared, just as the pain of those days eventually went away.

SANDY BLEIFER

Metal / Drawings

January 1997

The Metal / Drawings series is a combining of found metal parts with previously created charcoal, pencil, and ink drawings on newsprint or vellum from life drawing workshops. The figure drawings, which were done on very fragile papers implying the fragility of the human condition, were selected for their size and poses and paired with their metal counterparts. Some were placed behind metal screens to suggest imprisonment while others were supported by the metal as a means of providing strength and support, both practically and symbolically.

Most of these pieces were scorched and burned as a means of connecting the rust from the metal to the charcoal in the drawings. Newsprint darkens and becomes brittle over time, and burning made the paper even more fragile. These were qualities I wanted to juxtapose with the supposedly enduring qualities of metal. The truth is that the metal parts have continued to rust and deteriorate alongside the newsprint.

METAL / DRAWINGS I

9"W x 11-1/2"H x 2"D

Process Information: Found metal, pencil drawing and blood on vellum.

Concept: The contour drawing using graphite suggested the pairing with the metal mesh. Like some of the other drawings, this was originally over-painted with blood.

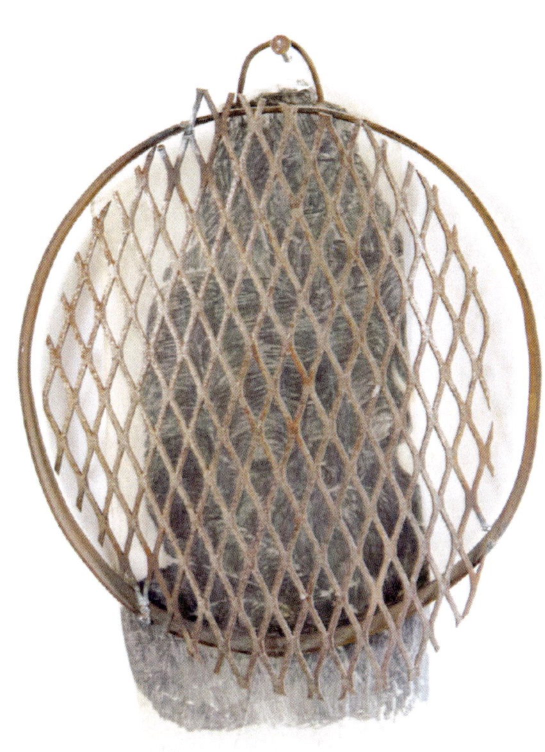

METAL / DRAWINGS II

21"W x 29"H x 1"D

Process Information: Charcoal on newsprint mounted on metal grate, burned.

Concept: The drawing is pressed into the front of the grate and burned so that the shapes of the grate behind are emphasized.

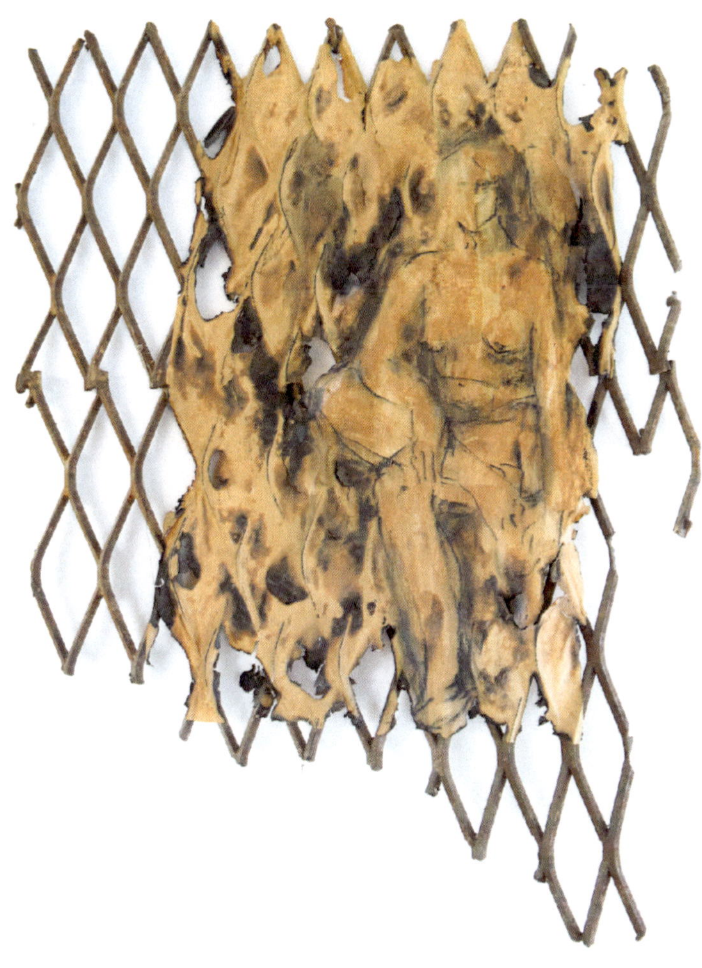

METAL / DRAWINGS III

17"W x 17"H x 1"D

Process Information: Charcoal on newsprint mounted on hubcap and burned.

Concept: The cross-legged pose of the model suggested a Buddhist meditation and a mandala form to the metal mounting. The piece was burned to make the drawing conform to the surface of the metal, revealing the open parts of the metal behind.

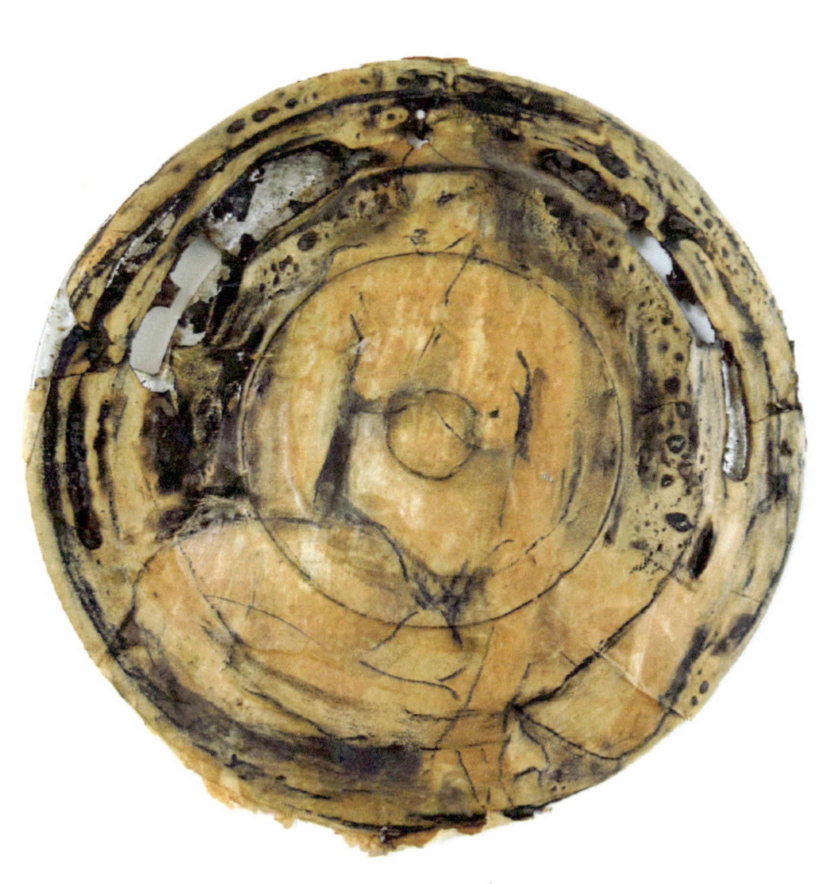

METAL / DRAWINGS IV

13"W x 17"H x 1-1/2"D

Process Information: Charcoal on newsprint mounted on perforated metal frame.

Concept: The drawing is attached to conform to the flat surface of the metal backing and is wrapped around the edges like a stretched canvas. The heavily rusted metal bled through to the face of the drawing. I hope this continues over time, further enhancing the bond between the drawing and its support.

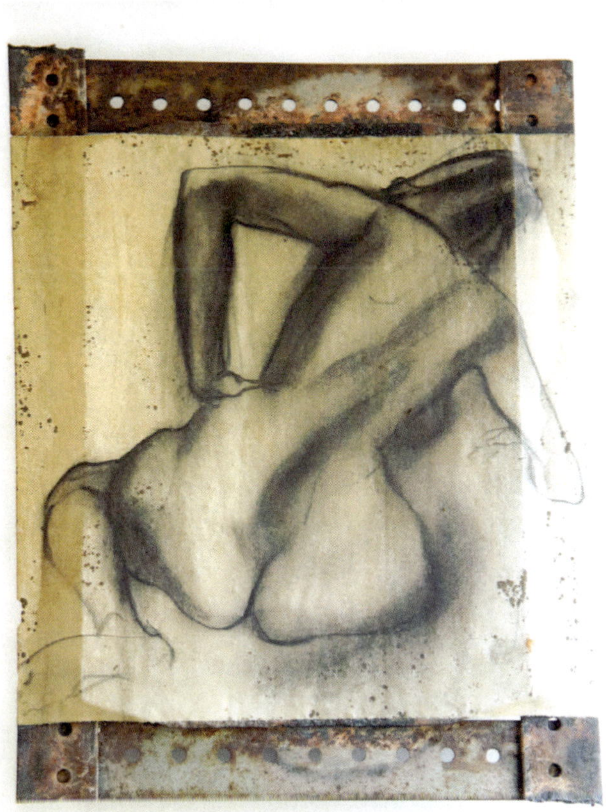

METAL / DRAWINGS V

13"W x 29"H x 1"D

Process Information: Charcoal on newsprint mounted behind a metal grid and burned.

Concept: The burning shows the vulnerability of the figure unprotected behind an open screen.

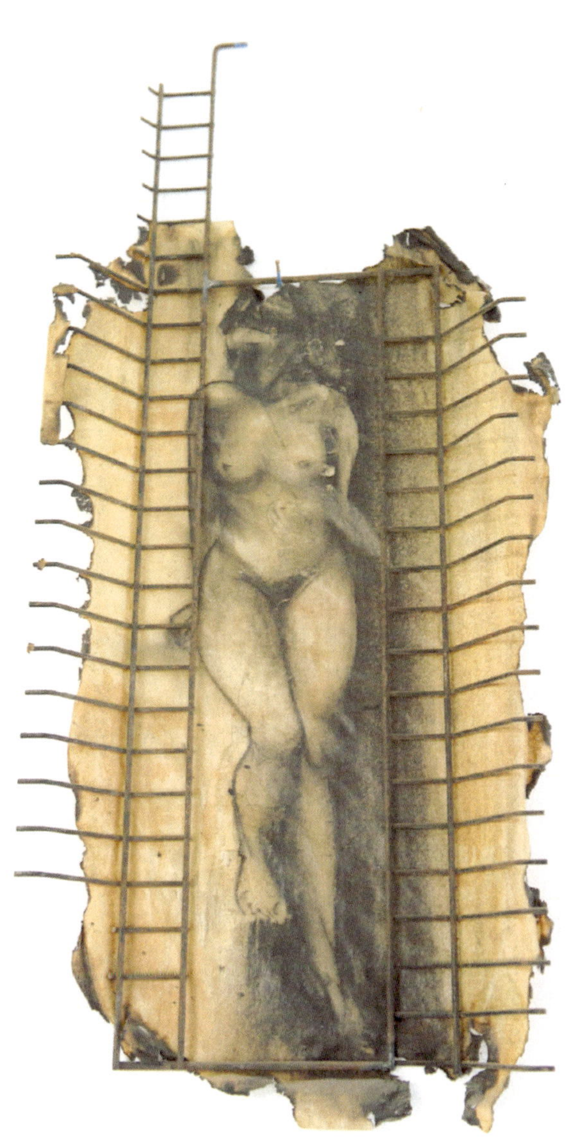

METAL / DRAWINGS VI

12"W x 12"H x 1"D

Process Information: Pencil on newsprint adhered to a rusted paint can lid.

Concept: This is a very minimalist drawing of a woman's buttocks adhered to very simple metal fragment. The roundness of the shape of the drawing and the lid reflect the rounded buttocks.

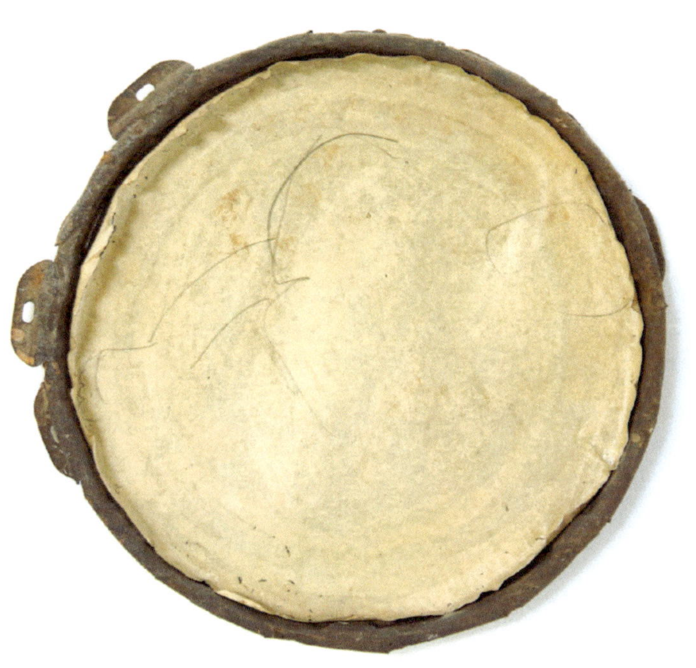

METAL / DRAWINGS VII

18"W x 36"H x 1"D

Process Information: Charcoal on newsprint mounted behind twisted metal bars and burned at the bottom edge.

Concept: The shape suggests that the person was held over an open flame by the ankles.

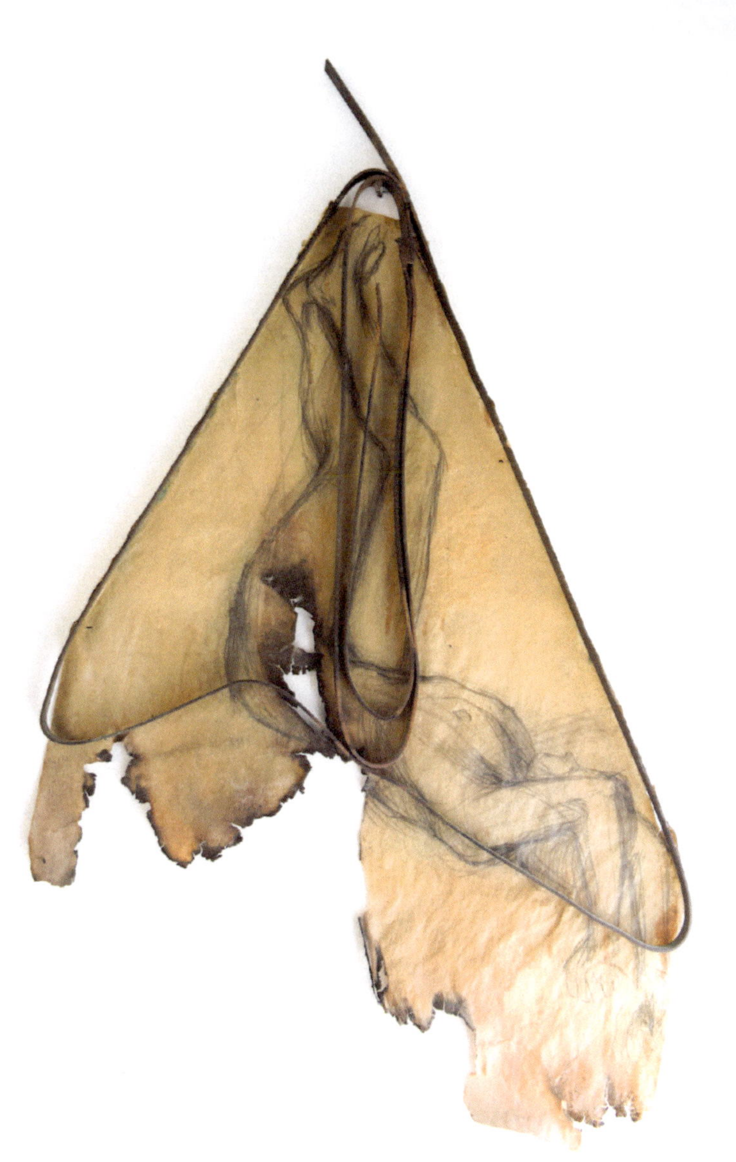

METAL / DRAWINGS VIII
13"W x 25-1/2"H x 1"D

Process Information: Charcoal on newsprint mounted behind a found metal grate.

Concept: The figure is completely confined behind bars and the gesture of her hands is also confining.

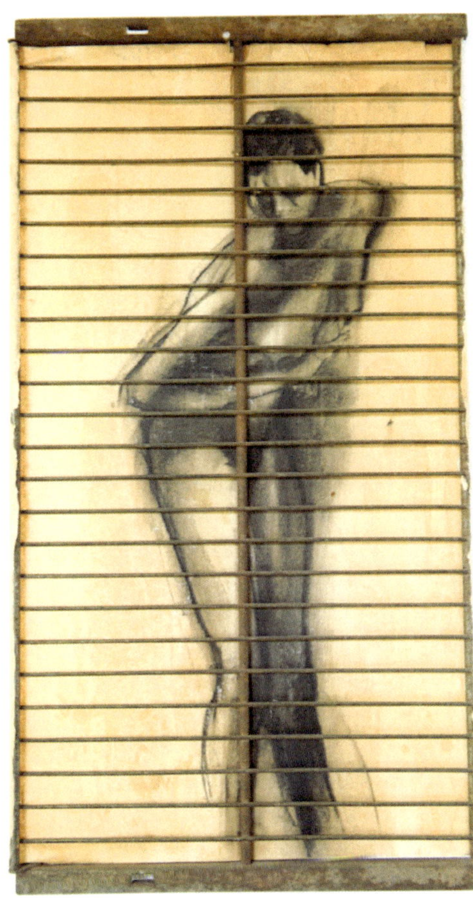

METAL / DRAWINGS IX

16"W x 10-1/2"H x 1"D

Process Information: Charcoal on newsprint, painted on the back with red acrylic, burned at the exposed edge and mounted to the back of a metal vent cover.

Concept: The extended part of the drawing reveals the feet. In order to see the rest of the figure, one needs to get up close to and below the vents in order to see the reclining figure inside. It is a voyeuristic piece.

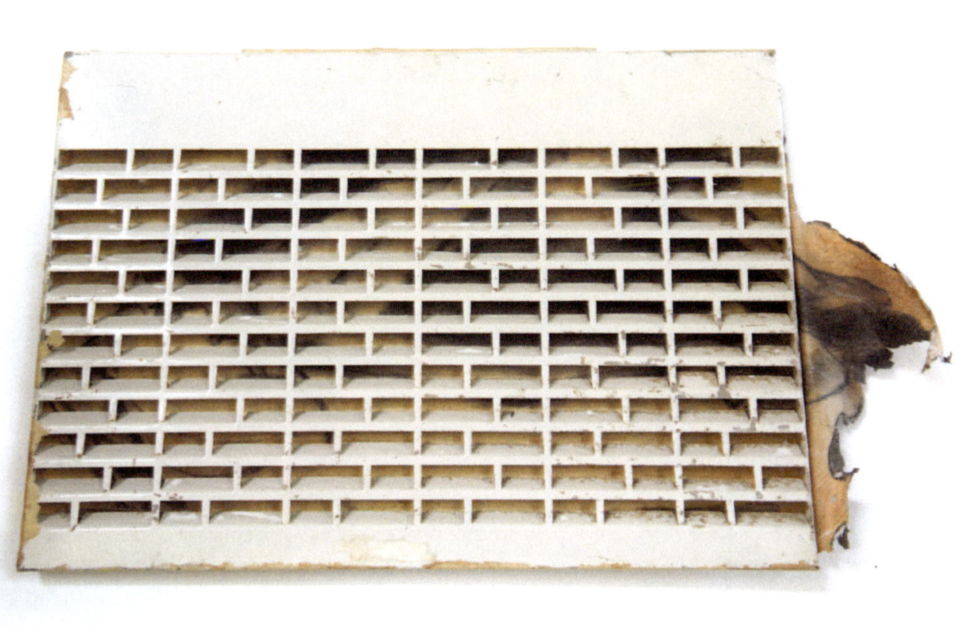

METAL / DRAWINGS X

11"W x 27"H x 2"D

Process Information: Charcoal drawing on vellum painted with my blood and burned then mounted on a cut out metal piece then wrapped in chicken wire. Like all the other drawings where blood was used as paint, the blood rapidly faded and is no longer visible

Concept: The gesture of the crossed legs suggests that the figure has been squashed between the pierced metal wall in front and the chicken wire mesh behind it.

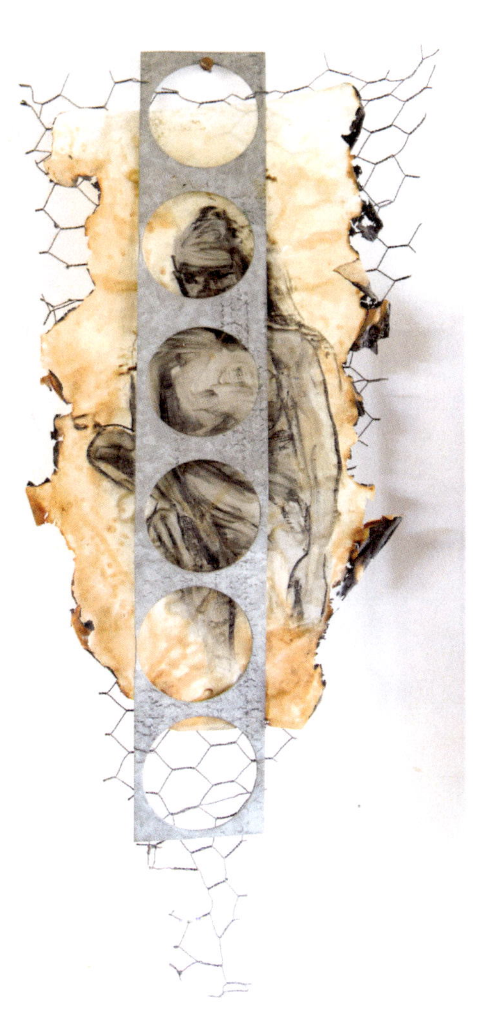

METAL / DRAWINGS XI
10"W x 14-1/2"H x 1"D

Process Information: Charcoal on vellum with part of the figure painted in blood (which has since faded) and burned, then mounted behind scrap metal parts.

Concept: The screw on the top of the metal arm seems to be bolting the figure in behind the screen.

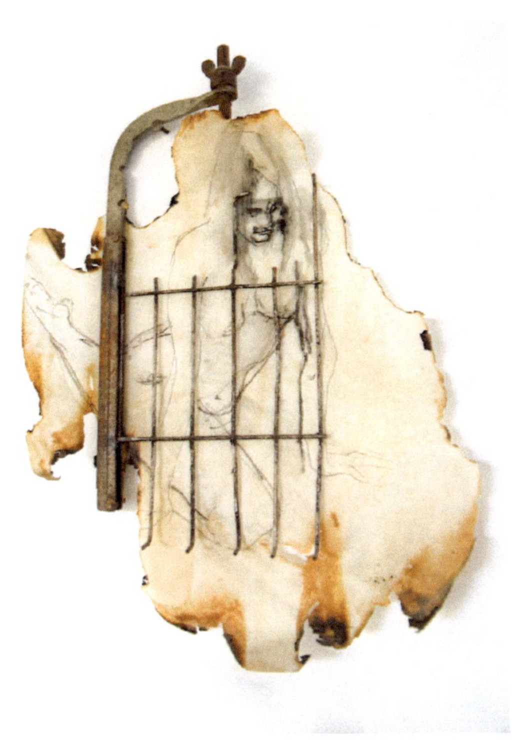

METAL / DRAWINGS XII

6"W x 15"H x 2-1/2"D

Process Information: Ink wash and blood painting of a figure on vellum, adhered to a curved piece of mesh screen and burned.

Concept: The curve of the mesh screen shapes the figure in 3-dimension and becomes the structural support for the burned skin of the body. Once the blood that defined many elements of the figure faded away, the drawing, literally, became a ghost.

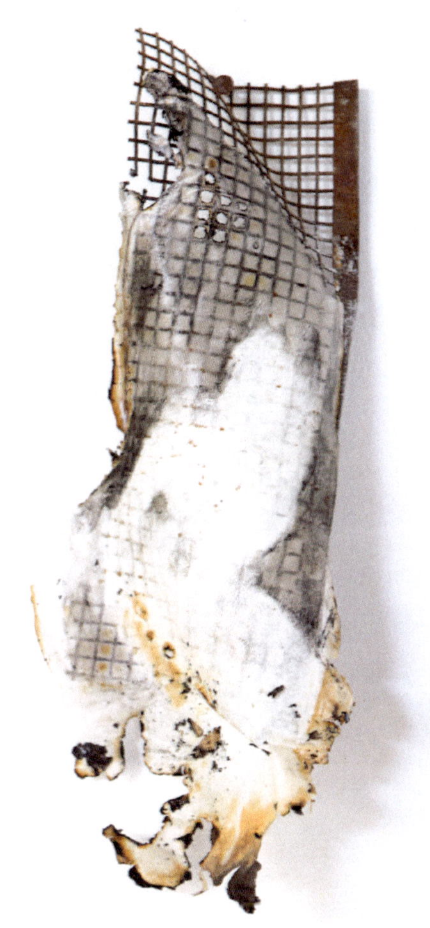

METAL / DRAWINGS XV
23"W x 12"H x 8"D

Process Information: Charcoal on newsprint adhered to a motorcycle fender and burned.

Concept: Functionally, the fender provided the support for the drawing and enabled it to round out in three-dimensions. Conceptually, draping a body around the fender represents the many injuries and deaths from motorcycle riding.

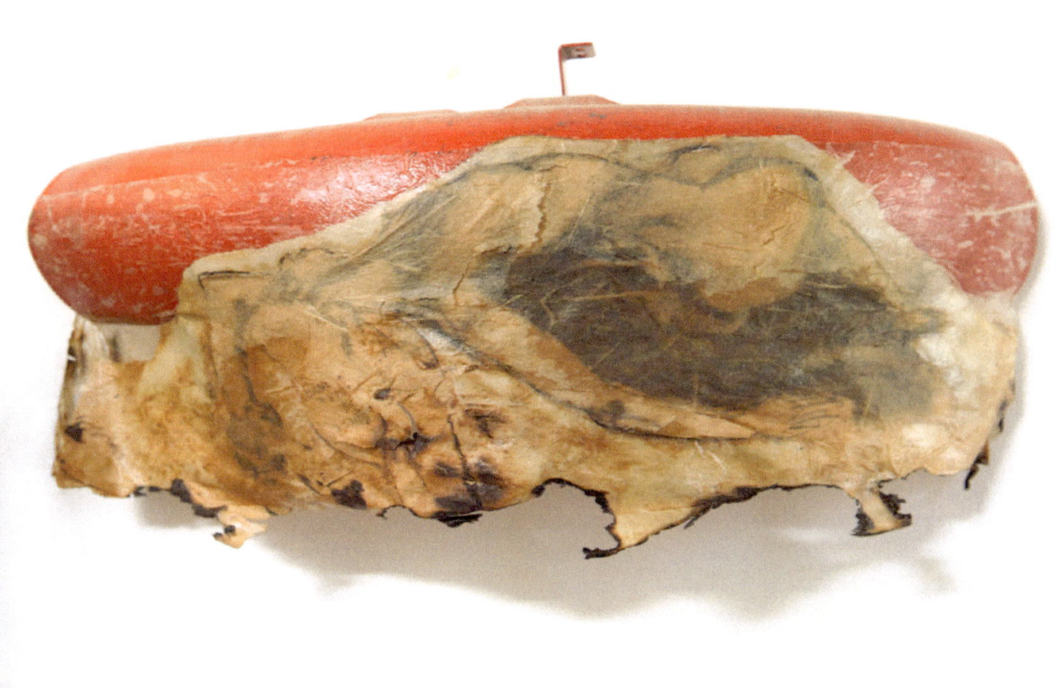

METAL / DRAWINGS XVI
9"W x 55"H x 5"D

Process Information: India ink on synthetic Japanese tissue mounted behind openings in a crushed bumper.

Concept: The India ink bled into fibers in the paper suggesting actual bleeding. The bumper is used to frame representations of the many people who die in automobile accidents.

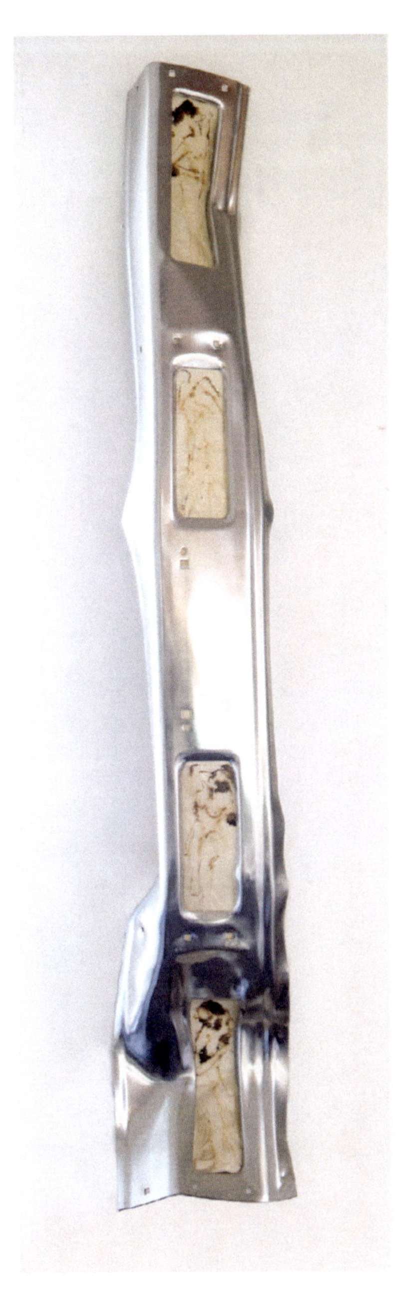
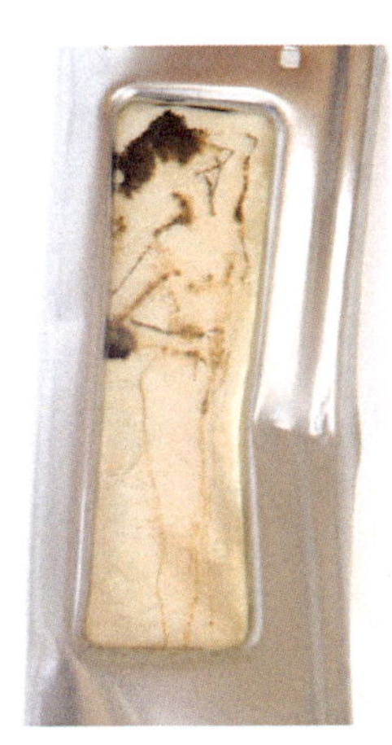
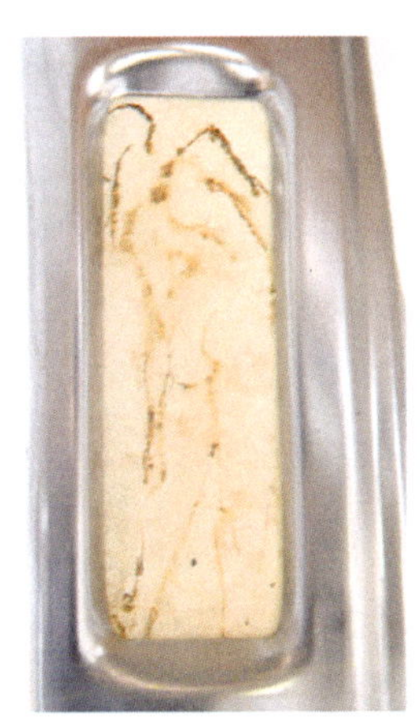
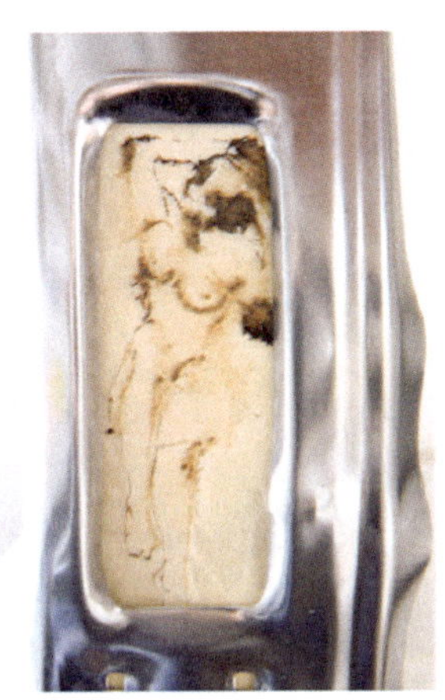
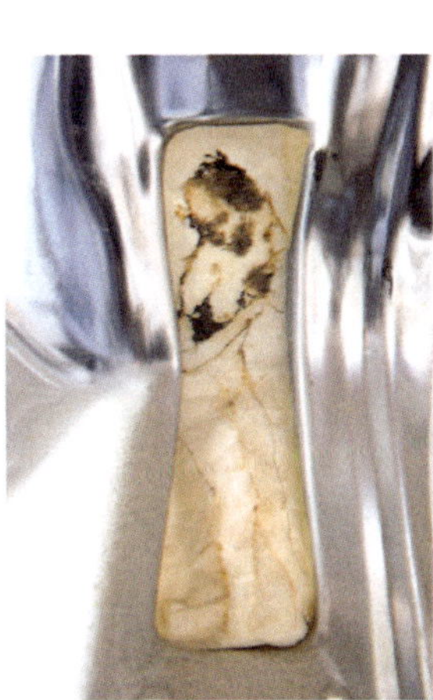

METAL / DRAWINGS XVII

5"W x 11"H x 1-1/2"D

Process Information: Graphite on tissue adhered to a metal plate.

Concept: The subtle contours of the metal plate add a 3rd dimension to the breasts and abdomen. This was intended to imitate a cast bronze statue of a partial figure.

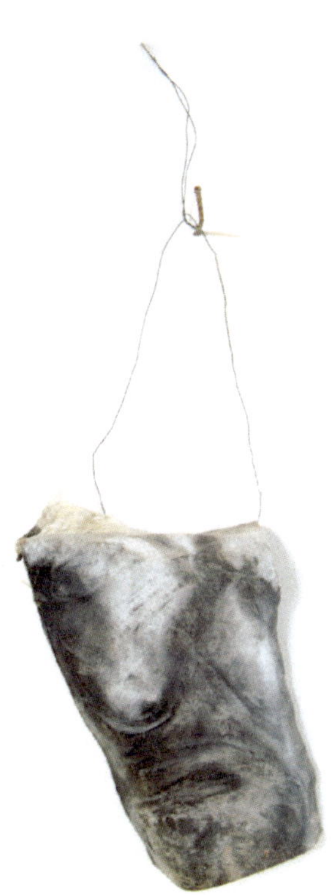

DEER HEAD

58"H x 18"W x 8"D

Process Information: Metal and tree bark/branches.

Concept: Sculpture out of scrap materials.

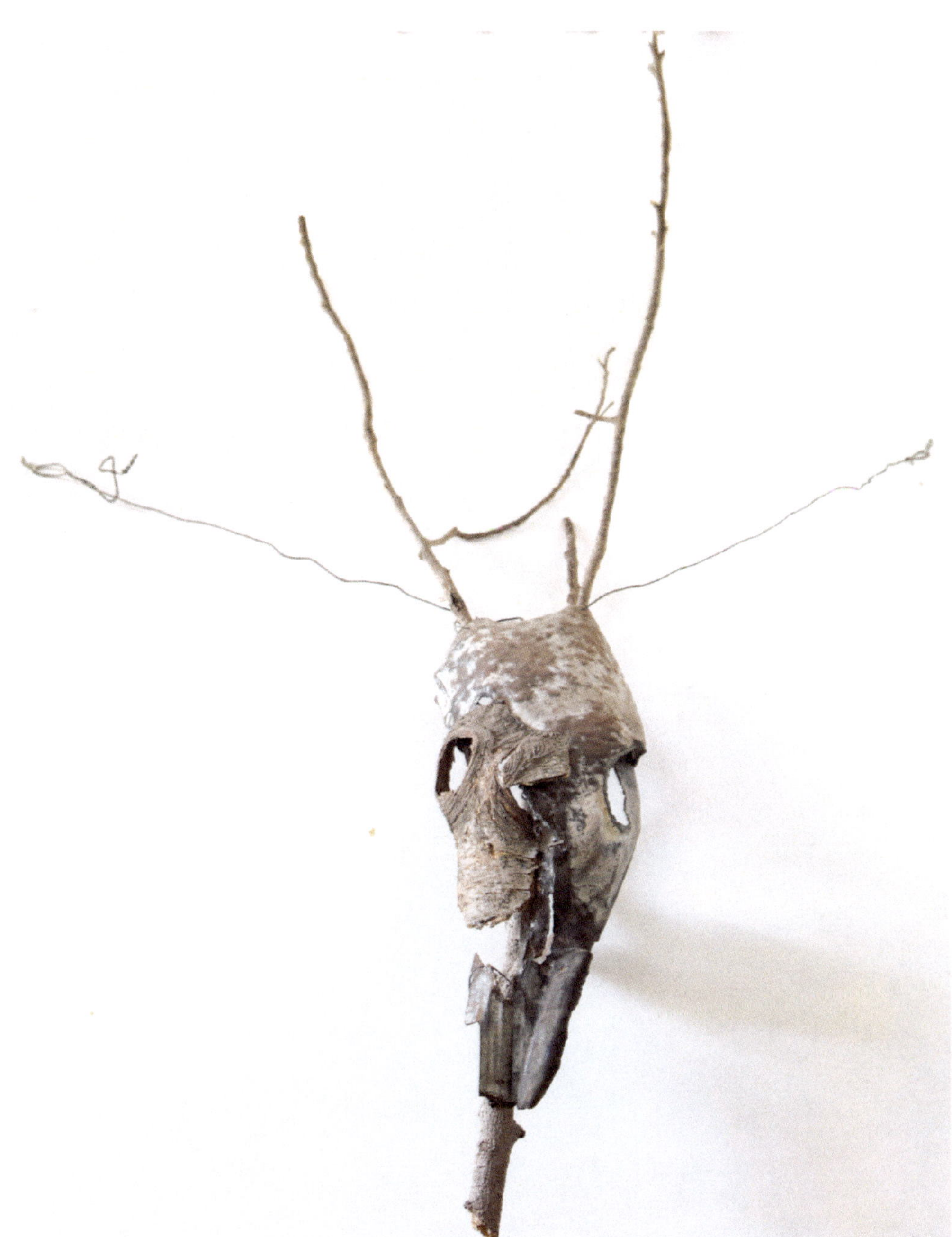

Palimpsest

*"something reused or altered but still bearing
visible traces of its earlier form"*

On January 5, 2016, a fire burned down artist and gallerist Flavio Bisciotti's home art studio. The loss included his personal paintings, photographs and ephemera, furniture, objects, tools, materials, clothing, files, and things he had collected over his lifetime.

After the initial shock and after speaking with friends, he came up with the idea to salvage the remains of the fire to create new artworks and present them in an exhibition. It was to be a collaborative community effort where fellow artists were able to make art from the ashes and to build relationships each other.

This project intrigued me on several levels: as a source of materials and media for bodies of work currently underway, as a transformative event that offered new creative direction for Flavio and the rest of us in the aftermath of destruction, and as testimony to the instinct for survival that is fundamental to the future of civilization.

IKEBANA XXV-A: FREESTYLE
(1st half of a diptych)
58"H x 13"W x 3"D

Process Information: Japanese hand made paper, art papers, scraps of all previous Ikebana pieces imbedded in cotton linters and abacca, twine and tassels.

Concept: In the rest of the Ikebana series, the part A of each diptych represented the perfection of the flower arrangement depicted. Since part B of this 25th and final pair of this series was developed first, part A was created based on the imagined arrangement of the flowers before the fire.

IKEBANA XXV-B: STUDIO FIRE
(2nd half of a diptych)
48"H x 13"W x 4-1/2"D

Process Information: Scorched and corroded ceiling light fixture and wires, dried curly willow and anthurium

Concept: When I saw the burnt light fixture at Flavio's studio it reminded me of a Tokonomo: the alcove in a Japanese teahouse used to display flowers and a scroll for the Tea Ceremony. The box holding the electrical mechanism of the fixture reminded me of the tall vases we use for Ikebana. What was missing was the flowers. Because the fixture (and, therefore, the alcove) had been burned and destroyed it was appropriate to use dead plant material. This piece became part of the final pair of diptychs in the Ikebana Series.

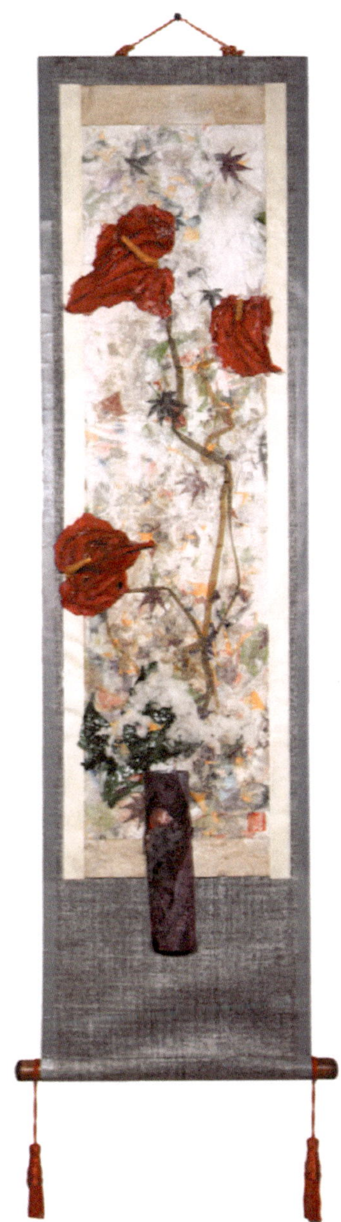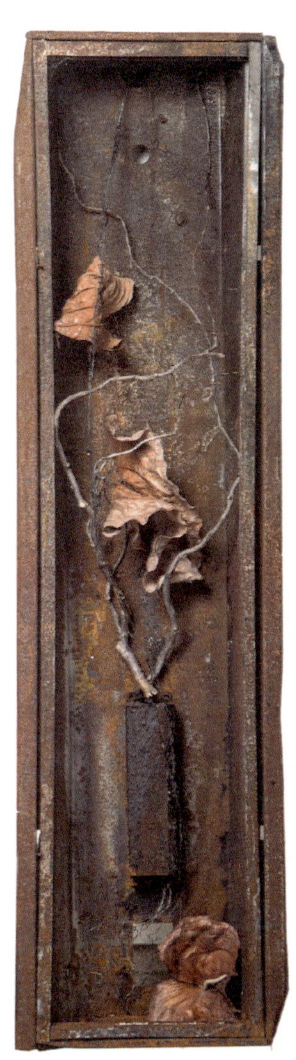

COFFIN: RISING FROM THE ASHES
48"H x 13"W x 4-1/2"D

Process Information: Scorched and corroded ceiling light fixture. Handmade paper (cotton linters and abacca) imbedded with Flavio Bisciotti's burned clothing formed in a mold taken of my back from my Holocaust Series, scorched with a propane torch. Newspaper photo. Installed at Flavio's studio on a pile of his burned clothing.

Concept: This is another interpretation of the object of the same ceiling light fixture used in Ikebana XXV-B: Studio Fire. By using the form of my body dressed in Flavio's burned clothes, I show my identification with and empathy for his situation, as all artists dread the destruction of their life's work.

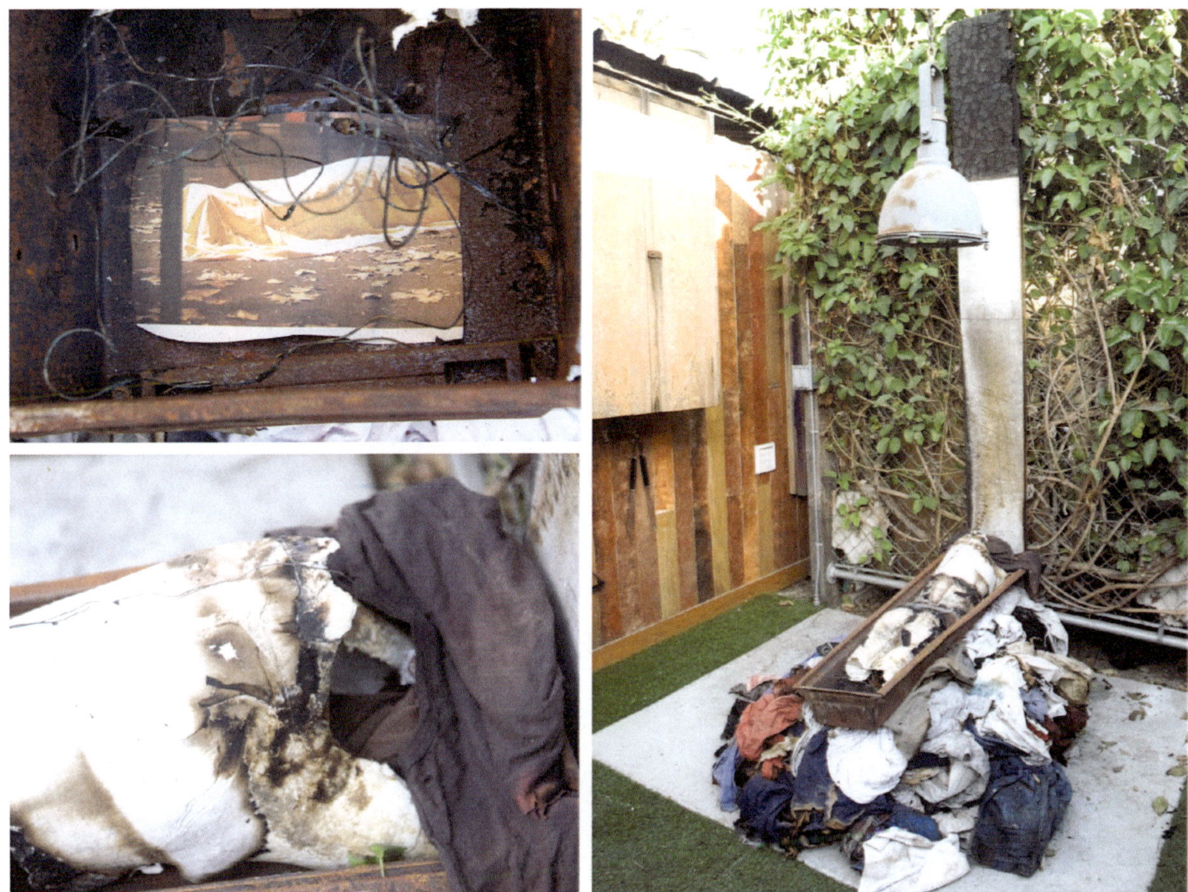

STATEMENT

I have always been concerned about destructive forces: man's inhumanity to man, the destructive forces of nature, the active role of human civilization as it impacts the environment, and the increasing polarization of society. Since my primary medium has been paper - not only as the surface for imagery, but as a painting and sculpting material - fire has become a mark-making tool as well as a process of sculptural reformation.

The subject matter of my work has changed over the past 40 years from landscape, architecture, urban environment, and nature to figurative imagery and social issues. Likewise, many of the expressive techniques have evolved to include burning, rust and other transient processes. Regardless of subject matter, these highly destructive methods push the limits of the paper's ability to survive, yet the paper endures. With my figurative work dealing with issues of the human condition, metal has become the perfect foil for paper. Metal, because it is so much more resilient to abuse than paper, stands in for the overwhelming forces of nature and society which humanity attempts to transcend. It is this inherent tension that defines modern society.

RESUME

Sandy Bleifer received her B.A. in Fine Arts at UCLA in 1962 and worked as an Artist in Residence for the Beverly Hills Schools as well as an art teacher, docent, and publisher of curriculum materials in the arts. Under the aegis of "Space", a seminal Los Angeles gallery under the direction of Edward Den Lau, she exhibited and sold her work from the early '70s through 1997 at many galleries and museums including the Downey Museum of Art, University of California, Berkeley, Loyola Marymount University, Mt. St. Mary's College, the Craft and Folk Art Museum, Riverside Art Museum, Chapman College, Palos Verdes Art Center and the art rental galleries of the Newport Harbor Art Museum, the San Francisco Museum of Art, and the Los Angeles County Museum of Art.

Her work is included in the collection of the Albuquerque Museum of Art, New Mexico, the Kitakamakura Museum, Japan and in many private and corporate collections including those of ARCO, IBM, Faberge, Neutrogena, and Security Pacific Bank. She is included in a recently published encyclopedia of Los Angeles artists before the 1980s, by Lyn Kienholz.

In 1975, the City of Los Angeles commissioned her to paint a mural on the Hayvenhurst underpass of the Ventura freeway. It can still be seen there and has been included in the definitive compendium of mural art in Los Angeles, Street Gallery by Robin J. Dunitz. Long a social activist, Bleifer concluded a six-year project to present her Hiroshima/Nagasaki Memorial Project to audiences in the U.S. and Japan in 1995. While becoming involved in the revitalization of the historic buildings and neighborhoods in downtown Los Angeles, she continued to evolve in new directions and is currently returning to painting in conjunction with collage and sculptural use of handmade papers.